Abracadabratude

Abracadabratude

Poems by

Chris O'Carroll

© 2021 Chris O'Carroll. All rights reserved.
This material may not be reproduced in any form, published,
reprinted, recorded, performed, broadcast,
rewritten or redistributed without
the explicit permission of Chris O'Carroll.
All such actions are strictly prohibited by law.

Cover art by Shay Culligan
Cover image by Alex Borland

ISBN: 978-1-63980-047-6

Kelsay Books
502 South 1040 East, A-119
American Fork, Utah 84003
Kelsaybooks.com

for NFE & AM

for AH & JB

Acknowledgments

Poems in this book have appeared (some in slightly different versions) in these print and online publications:

An Amaranthine Summer (anthology published in memory of Kim Bridgford): "Top of the First" (reprinted from *Life and Legends*)
Angle: "Chemistry," "Points in Space," "Public Service Announcement"
The Asses of Parnassus: "On a White Conceptual Poet's Performance of Michael Brown's Autopsy Report"
The Barefoot Muse: "Balcony Scene," "Making Light Among the Tombs," "Taste and See That the Lord Is Wrathful," "Wands and Cauldrons," "Zeus on Courtship"
Better Than Starbucks: "Good Enough Love Song"
Bit City Lit: "To a Defender of Poetic Tradition"
Blue Unicorn: "Tongue"
Chimaera: "Tall Tale"
Concise Delight: "After the Recent Scandal," "Remembering John Whatsisname"
14 by 14: "Till Death Do Us Part"
Free Inquiry: "Credo"
The Higgs Weldon: most of "Filmericks"
Life and Legends: "Top of the First"
Light: part of "Filmericks," "Monticello Updates the Exhibits," "Moose and Squirrel," parts of "Next Lines," "The Princess and the Pea," "Riyadh Reformer," "Toke Me out to the Ball Game," "Vampire Desire"
Lighten Up Online: "Disturbance in the Force," "Generations"
Literary Review: "Legend," "Owl and Pussy-Cat Honeymoon"
Love Affairs at the Villa Nelle: "Red and Gold"
The Oldie: "Tattooist's Tale"
The Orchards: "Arcadia's Peacocks"
The Rotary Dial: "Dali's Dials," "Searching for the Tree, San Fernando," "Sexiest Woman Alive"
Snakeskin: "Arab Spring Rubaiyat, 2011," "Family Meal," "Great American Novel Limerick," parts of "Next Lines," "No Comparison," "Theology," "Valentine's Day Triolet"

The Spectator: "Bard Bio Triptych," "Elementary," "Good Golly!" "Postcard from the Afterlife," "Strange Visitor," "Touch Acrostic," "Very Tragical Mirth"

Take These Rhymes . . . Please: Rude Limericks and Other Crimes Against Literature: "Bedtime Reading," "Curse You!" "How the West Was Wayne"

3rd Muse Poetry Journal: "How Many Poets Does It Take to Screw in a Light Bulb?"

Tilt-a-Whirl: "Ballade of the Bod," "The Reveal"

Uniquely Quabbin: "Red and Gold" (reprinted from *Love Affairs at the Villa Nelle*)

The Washington Post: part of "Supernatural Sitcoms"

"Tall Tale" appears in English and in Czech translation at the website Vybrané Překlady Básní z Angličtiny.

Three poems in this collection appear in the Potcake Chapbooks series—"Monticello Updates the Exhibits" in *Rogues and Roses,* "Tongue" in *Wordplayful,* and "Arab Spring Rubaiyat, 2011" in *Murder!*

Contents

Delicately Twisted

How Many Poets Does It Take to Screw in a Light Bulb?	17
In Praise of a Pandemic, 2020	18
Dramatic Genres	19
Strange Visitor	20
Tall Tale	21
Ode to a Dairy Product	22
To a Defender of Poetic Tradition	23
Tattooist's Tale	24
Credo	25
Toke Me out to the Ball Game	26
Arcadia's Peacocks	27
Legend	28
Dali's Dials	29
Postcard from the Afterlife	30
Next Lines	31
Generations	32
Dear Janis	33
Red and Gold	34
Remembering John Whatsisname	35
Arab Spring Rubaiyat, 2011	36
Ditch Lily	38
On a White Conceptual Poet's Performance of Michael Brown's Autopsy Report	39
Theology	40
Top of the First	41
Owl and Pussy-Cat Honeymoon	42
Vampire Desire	43
Elementary	44
The Princess and the Pea	45

Deep in Zero

Tongue	49
Chemistry	50
Sexiest Woman Alive	51
Public Service Announcement	52
Ballade of the Bod	53
The Reveal	54
Till Death Do Us Part	55
Valentine's Day Triolet	56
Searching for the Tree, San Fernando	57
After the Recent Scandal	58
Good Enough Love Song	59
Soul's Best Scent	60
No Comparison	61
Touch Acrostic	62

Abracadabratude

Wands and Cauldrons	65
Making Light Among the Tombs	66
Family Meal	67
Bedtime Reading	68
Ham and Caviar	69
Jack	70
Riyadh Reformer	71
Monticello Updates the Exhibits	72
How the West Was Wayne	73
Disturbance in the Force	74
Good Golly!	75
Curse You!	76
Points in Space	77

Moose and Squirrel	78
Very Tragical Mirth	79
Filmericks	80
Supernatural Sitcoms	82
Taste and See That the Lord Is Wrathful	83
Hairy Sibling Rivalry	84
Zeus on Courtship	85
Great American Novel Limerick	86
Melancholy Danish Limerick	87
Anonymous	88
Balcony Scene	89
Bard Bio Triptych	90

Introduction

Three stanzas into Chris O'Carroll's poem "Arcadia's Peacocks" we arrive at a false ending: the birds are a nuisance; their exotic excess is cloying and tiresome. The poem continues for three more stanzas before arriving at an altogether different conclusion, celebrating the "grace notes we/routinely discount," e.g., "dandelion anarchy" and "the chirping notes/night's peacock-ordinary crickets sing."

Readers of *Abracadabratude* will quickly realize why O'Carroll gave his peacock poem a second, more sympathetic ending. He, too, is prone to dazzling excess. Having written a sequel to "The Owl and the Pussy-Cat," he proceeds to update another light verse masterpiece, "Casey at the Bat." Not content to have written the devilishly clever monorhyme which bills itself as "A Postcard from the Afterlife," he adds a hybrid monorhyme/quatern, "Elementary," which requires finding twelve rhymes for "Mendeleev."

O'Carroll works magic with the unabashedly light forms of verse. His double dactyls are to die for. His limericks comment with equal authority on sitcoms and holy writ; others encapsulate Greek classics and American film classics; three linked limericks provide a brief but complete biography of William Shakespeare.

In the best poems in this collection, however, O'Carroll brings his light touch to bear on things about which he is quite serious. When he offers the reader his "Credo," he's not being ironic or facetious. He's not joking when, in his poem "Generations," he presents his self-portrait as "a paragon of immaturity."

And, clearly, this a poet who is seriously in love. The book's middle section is the performance of a lovestruck virtuoso: three Shakespearean sonnets, a sonnenizio, a rondeau redoublé, a triolet, an acrostic, a bawdy and exquisitely-crafted ballade . . . and "Till Death Do Us Part," a mere unrhymed sonnet which may be this collection's masterpiece. Its every syllable comes straight from the heart, wearing its dancing shoes.

Chris O'Carroll writes clever, funny verse, but don't let him fool you; he's one serious poet, a master craftsman with such a wealth of wit, I imagine him raising a glass with the gang at the Mermaid Tavern. Those Elizabethans would have welcomed him as a kindred spirit.

—Alfred Nicol, Author of *Animal Psalms*

Delicately Twisted

How Many Poets Does It Take to Screw in a Light Bulb?

Eschew the headlong thrust, but choose the screw,
That subtle swerve that Archimedes knew.
Let there be light by means of deft rotation
And delicately twisted penetration.

In Praise of a Pandemic, 2020

Earthquakes shatter California,
Twisters wrench at the Great Plains,
Every year the Gulf Coast suffers
New assaults from hurricanes.

With our far-flung friends and families,
We feel worries crowd our minds.
Mortal danger's extra scary
When we fear so many kinds.

Thanks to you, Covid-19, we
Now have less to keep track of—
Everywhere, just one convenient
Killer stalks the ones we love.

Dramatic Genres

Tragedy ends in death, they taught,
While comedy ends in sex.
Comedy *starts* with sex, I'd have thought.
The subject gets way complex.
Shakespeare sometimes tangles his plays
Where one genre intersects
Another. His characters' numbered days
As they get laid in elaborate ways
Continue to win him a few hoorays.

Strange Visitor

Yes. I remember Superman,
Originally called Kal-El,
A hero from another world
Who served Earth's human family well.

Our yellow sun endowed him with
Great speed and strength. Plus, he could fly.
No gun or bomb could injure him.
He beamed a heat ray from each eye.

His native world blew up. Its shards
Became a lethal green debris
That weakened him and pained him with
The specter of mortality.

We lack his powers, but this truth
He learned is one we also know:
Some fragments from our origin
Will find us everywhere we go.

Tall Tale

Might Frank Lloyd Wright have been wrong
When he surveyed the Depression-era New York City skyline and decreed that the Empire State Building didn't belong?
Speaking as one with more than average entitlement to his opinion about what does and does not rise to the level of architectural perfection,
Wright sneered, "Why thrill with the glint on an aluminum erection?"
(A disparaging remark whose carnal implications would reverberate soon thereafter in the thrilling, first-time antics of a giant cinematic ape
Palming a hot blonde and jungle-gymming up the skyscraper's by then already iconic phallic shape.)
The great architect went on to assail the tower with such epithets as "unethical monstrosity" and "piling up of wreckage by means of blind forces," which sounds inadvertently prophetic
To a world that has witnessed (in 2001, the year in which Wright's *bête noire* achieved the age of threescore and ten) the destruction of two younger, taller, uglier edifices by pilers up of wreckage whose quarrel with the buildings was not purely aesthetic.
But the point is, if an artist as eminent as Wright was mistaken, how much does it then behoove
The likes of you and me to cultivate the humble corrective of a few second thoughts regarding any new phenomenon of which we're initially inclined to disapprove?

Ode to a Dairy Product

Poets have been mysteriously silent on the subject of cheese
—G.K. Chesterton

For justifying God's ways, Stilton
Has the edge on malt and Milton.
No tongue can savor nor extol a
Rarer tang than Gorgonzola.

There is scarcely any food a
Gourmet ranks above aged Gouda.
Olympian deities all swear
They'd swap ambrosia for Gruyere.

Sublimest offspring of the dairy,
Oh, how thy scents and textures vary!
Such range of taste bud paroxysms
From milk and microorganisms!

Thou piquant source of stimulation
For palate and imagination,
Ancestral name of Python Cleese,
And stuff of classic sketch laughs—cheese!

To a Defender of Poetic Tradition

You know how people look like fools when they
Dis formal verse as fusty and passé?
When they call meter a straitjacket, rhyme
A lifeless fossil from a bygone time?
Well, that's how foolish you look when you damn
With cognate cluelessness the sins of slam.

You say slam poets seem to prize cheap thrills
And edgy topics more than verbal skills.
You grumble that they're all pierced, tattooed,
Unversed in subtle wordplay, "urban," crude.
Their hip-hop histrionics on the stage,
You sneer, can't match your deep thoughts on the page.

Thank God your coded ethnic slurs aren't cheap,
And your disdain for skin art is so deep.
The way you pierce the surface, plumb the core,
When you anatomize what you abhor
Saves you from sounding like some shallow jerk
With his head jammed up his collected work.

Are there particular slam poems you hate?
I might agree. I wouldn't hesitate
To say some slammers suck, if you'll admit
Page poets, too, sometimes write dreadful shit.
There's good work in both camps, and both include
Some poems as lousy as your attitude.

It's generally unwise to generalize
About whole genres when you criticize.
Keep it specific. Broad-brush imprecision
Makes you an easy target for derision.
Slammers, you charge, talk dirty. Which is true.
But so did Shakespeare. So do I. Fuck you.

Tattooist's Tale

Some ask for Chinese characters, which may
Or may not mean exactly what they think.
Some want a lover's name they can display
As skin-deep homage to a soulmate link.

Some, after passion's early glow is lost,
Are keen to have an ex's name erased.
They meet with laser surgeons, count the cost,
Then come to me to have the word replaced

Instead with twining tendrils, sleeves of flame,
Roses, skulls, angels, eagles, butterflies,
And other shapes I coax out of a name
As letters morph into their own disguise.

Young sweethearts, heed each fleeting whim's command.
Have *Carpe diem!* permanently wrought,
And put your trust in my transforming hand
When love (like Chinese) isn't what you thought.

Credo

I'm confident whatever gods may be
Don't think to be displeased or satisfied
With me, and don't expend their energy
On taking mine or any other side.

I'm confident the future and the past
Are present in this present we two share,
A moment that both does and doesn't last,
A here that's also somehow everywhere.

I'm confident that when mortality
Collects the tribute everybody pays,
We'll feel the fabric of eternity
As weightless as these evanescent days.

I'm confident that everything I know
Amounts to just a hunch or a rough guess.
I'm confident you'll hear the whole truth, though
The best words on my tongue say something less.

I'm confident that love is all we need.
Such trippy hippie wisdom cannot be
The only tenet of a lifetime creed,
Yet outweighs weightier philosophy.

I'm confident that your touch on my skin
Leaves its imprint on all of time and space.
I'm confident we're running not to win
Or lose or even comprehend the race.

Toke Me out to the Ball Game

*Major League Baseball (MLB) will remove marijuana
from its list of banned substances*
                    —*Reuters Sports News, 2019*

The outlook was, like, brilliant for the Weedville nine that day.
They vaped some prime sativa. Ergo, ultra-psyched to play.

When Weedville got the munchies, there was never any doubt
That vendors stocking Cracker Jack and peanuts would run out.

They ditched the anthem for a mellow dose of Grateful Dead.
The game was not a contest, but a work of art instead.

The physics of the knuckleball for once made perfect sense,
And home runs grokked the happy math of arcs above the fence.

A runner with a lead off first could slide through hyperspace
To wormhole past the tag and wind up safe at second base.

With Bolshoi Ballet grace the infield turned its double plays,
While journeyman outfielders were reborn as Willie Mays.

The talent was all Golden Glove, Cy Young, and Triple Crown,
So everybody got their tickets punched for Cooperstown.

The mojo of the game enacted cosmic majesty
As baseball truth converged and merged with baseball fantasy.

The players all flew higher than a patriotic eagle
In celebration of the news that cannabis was legal.

Arcadia's Peacocks

Peacocks have settled and adapted themselves to the City of Arcadia, particularly in the vicinity of the Arboretum. Although beautiful to view, peacocks can be a nuisance as well.
   —*arcadia.gov*

These are luxurious, exotic birds,
Showpieces of big-ticket decoration
On great estates. Here, though, an infestation,
Chewing through gardens, heaping lawns with turds,

Damaging roofs and ornamental trees
By perching well above a sparrow's weight,
Shrieking all night when it comes time to mate—
Loud, lusty, harem-seeking cocks, these peas.

They teach that even loveliest excess
Dulls to mere overdose, that every thrill
Can gag us with a cloying overkill,
Brewing toxicity from gorgeousness.

Or do they? Have we drawn the wrong conclusion
From spectacles we prize when they are rare
But grimace at when they swarm everywhere,
Lush beauties bloated to grotesque profusion?

Perhaps this bird turned commonplace invites
Attentiveness to mundane grace notes we
Routinely discount—silver energy
Whisking a supple squirrel's tail, gold highlights

Where dandelion anarchy zaps spring
And summer green, serene or frenzied motes
Surfing a daylight shaft, the chirping notes
Night's peacock-ordinary crickets sing.

Legend

My name is Slim or Curly
And I ride the open plains.
I'm plumb in love with horses
From their hooves up to their manes.

Spurs jingle at my boot heels,
A holster hugs my thigh.
My favorite year is yester
And my favorite noon is high.

A *cowpoke* some folks call me.
Shut up, I've heard the jokes.
I live on beans, black coffee,
Red-eye whiskey, hand-rolled smokes.

West Texas up to Abilene,
I smell like all outdoors.
Fragrance don't concern a man
Whose only dates are whores.

My hard hands give Chicago
And New York their tender steak.
The work is long and low-paid
And I squander what I make.

Beneath the starry Western sky
I lay my restless head.
You can catch me in the movies
Decades after I am dead.

Dali's Dials

after The Persistence of Memory

Can time stand still, or run, or creep?
Can it maintain one constant pace?
How does the mind flex, deep asleep,
To reconfigure time and space?

Clock faces soften, melt, and ooze.
One drapes a semi-human face.
Their mutable outlines refuse
To validate the commonplace.

When rigid shapes we think we know,
Rendered with hyper-real precision,
Can nonchalantly shift and flow,
Lifelike and dreamlike are one vision.

A timepiece swarms with ants, as though
It were, like flesh, prey to decay.
Thus art's subversive undertow
Whisks mere reality away.

Postcard from the Afterlife

How cool is Heaven? Where do I begin here?
The nightlife's hipper than pre-war Berlin here,
Yet wholesome as a cozy country inn here.
I'm suave as Cary Grant or Errol Flynn here.
I've got broad shoulders and a dazzling grin here,
Plus perfect hair, flat abs, and strong, cleft chin here.
(We all look like some sexy film star's twin here.)
Nobody hates the color of your skin here.
Yang enjoys perfect harmony with yin here.
The food is rich, yet all of us stay thin here.
Nobody has to lose for me to win here.
We're all on friendly terms with all our kin here.
No politicians practice crooked spin here.
I never get hung over from the gin here.
None of my favorite vices is a sin here.
Damned if I can tell how I got in here.

Next Lines

To see a World in a grain of sand
Is a trick that acidheads understand.
                    —Mike Bailwall

Much have I travell'd in the realms of gold.
Check out the blonde in this month's centerfold.

That's my last Duchess painted on the wall,
And over here's my life-size blow-up doll.

I wandered lonely as a cloud,
Being somewhat modestly endowed.

When in disgrace with fortune and men's eyes,
I hope the jury buys my lawyer's lies.

Something there is that doesn't love a wall,
Though you will want one if you play handball.

I hear America singing, the varied carols I hear,
Hymns to the flag, Mom, and baseball, anthems for hotdogs
    and beer.

Hope is the thing with feathers.
Spike is the dude in leathers.

Generations

At family get-togethers, who's the gray
Uncle who shocks the aunts with ribald jokes,
Then asks the twentysomethings if he may
Join them outside for newly legal smokes?

What slipper'd pantaloon sprawls on the floor
Beneath a squirming, giggling toddler scrum?
Whose silly magic tricks are not meant for
The grown-ups? *Look, he's pulling off his thumb!*

Who has no aptitude for adult games,
But, when the children make up goofy super-
Heroes, whoops with them as they shout their names?
I'm Booger Man! I'm Super Duper Pooper!

This foolish fellow who won't act his age,
This paragon of immaturity
Who thinks that all the world's a vaudeville stage,
Who's this absurd relation? Oh, it's me.

Dear Janis

after Leonard Cohen

I remember you well in the Chelsea Hotel
That alternative universe day.
On my knees by your bed, I was giving you head,
And you showed me you liked it that way.

You shot junk in your veins, I was tripping my brains
Out that decade. We both rolled the dice.
You went on to die young while my heart and my tongue
Went on playing with virtue and vice.

I don't mean to pretend there's some way to defend
All the ways I behaved in my youth.
I was so self-involved that I left unresolved
All our questions, our lies, and our truth.

Red and Gold

Flamboyantly decked out in red and gold—
Mellow and misty, yes, but something more—
The year grows gaudier as it grows old.

Before warm breath succumbs to winter cold,
Motley appears from a defiant store
Of finery, flamboyant red and gold.

This late extravagance was not foretold
By all the brilliant boutonnieres spring wore.
The year grows gaudier as it grows old.

Summer's mature green kept a steady hold,
Serenely continent awhile before
Fall's carnival excess of red and gold.

Threescore and more around the sun I've rolled.
Each autumn's frenzy calls me to explore
A madcap gaudiness as I grow old.

That bell time tolls will soon enough be tolled.
I'm primed for this unsubtle metaphor,
For some flamboyant notes of red and gold
To lend a gaudy grace to growing old.

Remembering John Whatsisname

Here's one whose name was writ in H_2O,
And here's a stone set up to tell us so.
Water will write the epitaph of stone,
And words endure, though transient to the bone.

Arab Spring Rubaiyat, 2011

The People rise and fling a Noose of Light
To snare and topple their dark Lord of Night.
The Tyrant sees the breaking Dawn and feels
His own Grip loosen as the Noose pulls tight.

The Vine of Liberty perfumes the Air
With fragrant Grapes whose Juice helps Dreamers dare
Great Things. Democracy is heady Wine.
Come dance! The Wine is flowing in the Square!

The Zeitgeist dips its Pen in Joy and Rage
To write this hopeful Drama on the Page.
As Players enter for their next Scene, will
The Ink be spilled as Blood upon the Stage?

This Generation chanting in the Street
Relies on Cyber-Playthings to unseat
The Autocrats whose Doom is spelled out in
140 Characters per Tweet.

A Book, a Loaf, a Jug—Youths might desire
These Luxuries, but All that they require
Is Access to the Websites where they seize
And reprogram this Scheme of Things entire.

Rulers whose Yokes have made their People groan
Now reap the Discontent their Crimes have sown.
They're baffled by the Speed with which Unrest
Updates their Facebook Status: overthrown.

Do doubtful Watchers in the West recoil
From certain Portents of Today's Turmoil?
Don't get us wrong, we love your Freedom, but
There's Something we love even more—your Oil.

Some Pundits theorize the Internet
Rewrites the Script such that Blood, Tears, and Sweat
Need not attend a Rising in this Age.
But wait. The Guns may have their Hour yet.

Ditch Lily

Cool in the blossom's throat, a yellow glow,
A molten, mellow gleam, wells harmlessly,
Yet tawny petals wear a dark, singed scar,
And at their crinkling edges seem to know
Some heat that rises like a scorching sea
To smudge its shore with this flame-licked-brick char.
Green leaves gulp sunlight. Roots gorge in the dark.
A cup the cousin of a monarch's wing
Shines in its depths. A surge of golden tide
Shoulders dirt tones aloft to leave their mark
Where the corolla arches everything,
Backbends the lily, curls it open wide,
A day-long emblem of its place of birth
Between the fire-fed sky and worm-turned earth.

On a White Conceptual Poet's Performance of Michael Brown's Autopsy Report

That was the Goldsmith poem that wasn't.
Black lives matter. Ken's crap doesn't.

Theology

Five senses, changing seasons, science, art,
The intricacies of the mind and heart—

Life's rife with miracles. It would be odd
If we were not moved to imagine God.

From what stuff, though, do we concoct God's will
Concerning food, drink, sex, and who to kill?

Top of the First

I will fling so fast, so crafty
That your strongest swing must fail.
The blow I wield, precise and mighty,
Lets no throw of yours prevail.

Before the straining runner's gait,
The grass-stained dive, the dust-cloud slide,
Our stances here define the contest—
Wit vs. strength on either side.

Owl and Pussy-Cat Honeymoon

"Our courtship was fun, now the wedding is done,
And we've issues we need to discuss,"
Said the Pussy. "Coition in any position
Is a knotty dilemma for us.
Never mind procreation, just plain recreation
Involving a cat and a bird
Looks to be heavy weather. Between fur and feather
Congress must, alas, prove absurd."

"My sweet wife," the Owl said, "our marital bed
Is a place we have no need to fear.
We were made for romance; we are creatures of fancy.
How pleasant to know Mr. Lear!
How do you suppose that a ring from the nose
Of a piggy fits snug on your paw?
Nonsensical verse can make better from worse.
We are not bound by natural law.

"We can dance hand in hand on the edge of the sand,
Though of hands we are neither possessed.
I strum my guitar, croon how lovely you are,
And the Muses take care of the rest.
Details of anatomy simply don't matter. We
Transcend such stuff; we belong
To a realm whose carnality scoffs at reality.
Come inhale from this tree; it's a Bong."

Vampire Desire

Though A is delicious, and B is nutritious,
While AB is rich and complex
Like a vintage Bordeaux, undead epicures know
That type O is better than sex.

Ask any *au fait* Transylvanian gourmet.
No drug that a junkie injects
Provides half the pleasure of this ruby treasure,
For type O is better than sex.

O is more than OK. OMG, O's *Olé!*
It's O that I want from your necks.
To you mortals, "big O" is the best, but I know
That type O is better than sex.

Elementary

Raise a toast to Dmitri, the great Mendeleev
And the atoms he charted his famous array of,
All the stuffs that all stuff's the ornate interplay of
On landscapes he helped us decipher the lay of.

Toast the pale pastel leisure-wear hues and the grey of
This table (bulked up a bit since Mendeleev),
Where groups abut periods stacked like parfait of
The properties they illustrate a buffet of.

Toast element 1, hydrogen, that mainstay of
The cosmos, then toast the split-second decay of
The heaviest yet in the scheme Mendeleev
Might not have imagined the long-lasting sway of.

In the patterns he choreographed his ballet of,
Element 118 makes the latest display of
The truth that today's the enduring heyday of
These columns and rows that recall Mendeleev.

The Princess and the Pea

The prince says, "The princess I'm hoping to wed,
The girl who, for me, has it all,
Is one who knows how to get worked up in bed
Over something incredibly small."

Deep in Zero

Tongue

The voice of a dog, the skin of a tree,
To injure one's shin—the word is the same.
Likewise a vessel for sailing the sea.
Four distinct concepts embraced by one name.
One word means journey or stumble and fall;
Just one suffices for trousers and gasps;
Woo, an arena with baskets and ball;
Drum with a fist, sixteen ounces of mass;
A role in a play, a line in one's hair;
Foliage, takes off; a corner, to fish;
Spades, hearts, clubs, diamonds, an outfit to wear;
Intelligent, sting; play tenpins, a dish.
We're stretched on this bed and yet I speak true:
I'm deep in zero in tennis with you.

Chemistry

sonnenizio on a line from Kim Addonizio's "So What"

Guess what. If love is only chemistry
(which I'd guess you believe and don't believe),
If we're the body's passive banquet guests
Until the menu serves its biggest treat
To help our flesh guess what dessert we crave,
Anyone on the guest list ought to do.
Why does my hand demand your leg, esteem
Your ass alone, as if all Vargas Girls,
All Playmates, guest-starred in your skin? With just
The vaguest notions about molecules
Spinning my brain and balls, how can I guess?
Hazard your best wild guess. Be my lab mate,
I beg. Essential experiments combine
All of your finest guesswork with all of mine.

Sexiest Woman Alive

*I think the risk of being the sexiest woman alive
is that you don't want to ever have sex again.*
                        —Kate Beckinsale

That's how the star responded when *Esquire*
Named her the world's prime object of desire.

In the event you feel likewise, I ought
To hasten to assure you that you're not.

(It wouldn't be the only time a guy
Had angled for some action with a lie.)

Or maybe, to incline you toward congress,
I'll say you are, but not inform the press,

The better to enjoy in blissful privacy
All of your sexiest woman alivecy.

Public Service Announcement

Ideally, this embrace would be
Just me for you and you for me.
Even if we assumed we could,
There would be no necessity

To bruit, *Hey, world, love is good!*
That would be widely understood,
Would shine in several billion eyes.
But as things stand, we feel we should

Go public, skywrite, advertise
What would be private otherwise,
The corny, horny truth that two
Becoming one can symbolize.

Just you for me and me for you—
If we asserted that we screw
For world peace, it would not be true.
And yet we do, we do, we do.

Ballade of the Bod

You know each separate part; you know the whole.
You make the world stand still; you make it spin.
Your every kiss ignites an aureole
With which plain virtue glows like garish sin.
If sex is a grenade, you pull the pin.
You take aim at me from that grassy knoll
Where all conspiracies end and begin.
Your body maps the contours of my soul.

Yours is the stage on which I play the role
Of bright-rubbed lamp and wonder-working djinn,
Yours the enchanted alley where I bowl
And get sent sprawling like a candlepin.
Who needs the journals of Anaïs Nin
If I may dip my quill and sign your scroll?
You stoop to conquer like a peregrine.
The contours of your body map my soul.

You are the goalie opening the goal
And welcoming the score when both teams win,
The chef whose oven heats this casserole
Of yang enfolded in sweet, spicy yin,
The bracing shot of high-proof, brand-name gin
That makes my breath halt and my eyeballs roll,
My mirthful kith and my most solemn kin.
Your contours map my body and my soul.

Prints of your touch that linger on my skin
Like ferns imparting life's own warmth to coal
Remind the flesh that it's the spirit's twin.
Our bodies map the contours of the soul.

The Reveal

It makes me giddy every time I see
You slip out of your garments to reveal
This blessedly familiar luxury,
This shrine at which I pray you'll let me kneel.

The most accomplished thief could never steal
A treasure rich as your largesse to me.
So fair a vista, dare I think it's real?
It makes me giddy every time I see

This Promised Land exceeding prophecy.
No starving beggar ever craved a meal
From which he hoped for half the ecstasy
You slip out of your garments to reveal.

No avid gambler wagers at the wheel,
No race car driver speeds through a Grand Prix
Envisioning a prize with more appeal—
This blessedly familiar luxury.

No oracle has framed an augury
That devotees embrace with keener zeal.
It snares my flesh and sets my spirit free,
This shrine at which I pray you'll let me kneel.

The secret that you choose not to conceal
Is, every time, a fresh discovery.
Glad choreographies we waltz and reel
Deplete yet multiply my energy.
It makes me giddy.

Till Death Do Us Part

To mention death might seem a bit perverse
On such a joyous day. But this day's joy,
Because it's death-defined, is death-defying.
About tomorrow, all we know for sure
Is that one day there won't be one for us.
Today might be our only yesterday
(Or yesterday might be). Yet every day,
Your hand in mine's a second certainty,
Pledging a sure thing no less sure than that.
Perhaps there should be some less doomstruck way
To say how much these vows mean. Please accept
My clumsy mortal thanks that I have found
In this embrace that can't last long enough
So much to live for and so much to lose.

Valentine's Day Triolet

I'm yours! You're mine! Hooray, hooray!
The same old message every year,
The same old glad glow on display.
I'm yours! You're mine! Hooray, hooray
For Valentine's Day games we play,
Games full of bare skin and good cheer!
I'm yours! You're mine! Hooray, hooray!
Same message this year, every year.

Searching for the Tree, San Fernando

The high rims of this valley fringe the blue
With every shape and shade of green. No way
To count the trees, nor to explain why you
Felt such a summons from that one. All day,
With lizards and songbirds for our companions,
We two explored the routes up that tree's slope
Through bougainvillea and orange blossom canyons
Colored and scented likewise with your hope
That every time we came around a bend
We'd have our moment of discovery.
We share this payoff at our journey's end:
We're back down in the valley, where the tree
We never reached crowns the horizon still.
We hold hands, gaze together up the hill.

After the Recent Scandal

Some pols, so I hear tell, pay a gal a grand
An hour for all the stuff that you do for fun.
Your skin swaps untold wealth with my empty hand,
Freely splurging this fortune we've freely won.

Good Enough Love Song

Thank you for settling for me, darling.
That's just what I was hoping you would do.
Though I know I am not God's gift to women,
God knows I might be good enough for you.

Time was when we both hankered for perfection—
Some combination swimsuit model/saint,
But nowadays you do a lot of loving
In spite of everything this lover ain't.

You settled for me like it all was settled
We both would be OK somehow, some way.
Give me another dose of your good loving.
Who knows, I might be good enough one day.

I'm grateful you're the one that settled for me
When other girls had better things to do.
Darling, you're some kind of gift from Heaven,
So here on Earth, I'm good enough for you.

Soul's Best Scent

It's a raw breed of joy with a girl and a boy,
And you make it feel like a sacrament,
Which goes to show what you're sure to know—
Flesh lives to sniff out the soul's best scent.

No Comparison

Shall I compare thee to a kangaroo?
Shall I compare thee to a saxophone?
Shall I compare thee to a barbeque?
Shall I compare thee to a cornerstone?
Shall I compare thee to a minaret?
Shall I compare thee to a Muscadet?
Shall I compare thee to the internet?
Shall I compare thee to the Milky Way?
Shall I compare thee to a limousine?
Shall I compare thee to a powder horn?
Shall I compare thee to a trampoline?
Shall I compare thee to a unicorn?
Shall I compare thee to a simile
For dumbstruck love and half-mad fantasy?

Touch Acrostic

Across the qwerty keyboard of my heart
Strike digits briskly spelling out desire,
Desire your smallest tap-tap will jump-start,
For your touch is the type my nerves require.

Good loving is a nimble-fingered game.
Have at me with your practice and precision.
Jolt me in high-speed bursts with pinpoint aim.
Key in coordinates for sweet collision.

Let orthographical dexterity
Zestfully spell allure in every line,
X-rating to the last extremity,
Collating your adult consent with mine.

Vistas of romance open to your skill.
Bonanzas of love's wordplay multiply.
Neatly your click-clack crafts an unkempt thrill.
My pulse surrenders as your fingers fly.

Abracadabratude

Wands and Cauldrons

Hogwarts Academy
Headmaster Dumbledore,
Mentoring teens in four
Wizard school dorms,

Keeps a keen eye on their
Abracadabratude
As they brave occult and
Hormonal storms.

Making Light Among the Tombs

What if the grave were an
Evitability?
Verses might yet flow from
Anthony Hecht.

Still, his mortality
Fostered such lively wit,
It's a dead cert he knew
What to expect.

Family Meal

Loppety-choppety,
Titus Andronicus,
Self and kin hacked up by
Plotters malign,

Caters a banquet of
Grand Guignol payback, cries,
Anthropophagical
Vengeance is mine!

Bedtime Reading

Hookery-bookery,
Xaviera Hollander
Flexes her talent for
Turning a trick.

Specialized exercise
Regimens keep her a
Pubococcygeus
Muscle-bound chick.

Ham and Caviar

Shake-a-leg, break-a-leg,
Laurence Olivier
Chews on the scenery
Treading the boards.

Fearlessly overwrought
Theatricality
Makes him a thespian
Prince among Lords.

Jack

Whamalot-bamalot,
Jacqueline Bouvier
Marries a pol with a
Penchant to stray

(Just like his star-shagging
Paterfamilias).
His Monroe Doctrine is
She's a great lay!

Riyadh Reformer

Dynasty-phantasy,
Saudi Arabia
Frowns on corruption, we
Now come to learn.

This ain't his grandfather's
Kleptotheocracy.
Crown Prince got money and
Cousins to burn.

Monticello Updates the Exhibits

Liberty-flibberty,
Hemings and Jefferson
Made an arrangement in
Black, white, and gray.

Master/slave congress proved
Philoprogenitive.
Also consensual?
Harder to say.

How the West Was Wayne

"Three rules to live by," says
Marion Morrison:
"Monosyllabic names
Suit tough guys best,

Cinematography
Salvages one-note stars,
Rewritten history
Rules the Old West."

Disturbance in the Force

Afterlife Jedi pals
Yoda and Obi-wan
High-five a host of new
Stories to tell:

"Here's to the franchise's
Skywalkerectomy!
Let spinoffs spin till the
Freezing of Hell."

Good Golly!

Tutti-bam! Fruiti-boom!
Richard Wayne Penniman
Hollers it ribald and
Bangs it out blue,

Rocking America's
Youth to new rhythms of
Erotogenical
Wop-bop-a-loo!

Curse You!

Pocketa-pocketa,
Baron von Richthofen
Bellows, "I make foreign
Air aces swoon!

What do I care for the
Anthropomorphism
Charles Schultz promotes with his
Beagle cartoon?"

Points in Space

for JBC

Charting geometries
Post-Lobachevskian
Helps keep us yogically
Limber of mind.

Sketches of parallels
Extra-Euclidian
Stretch our perceptions past
Lines of one kind.

Moose and Squirrel

Badenov-hadenov,
Rocky and Bullwinkle,
Frostbite Falls spy foilers,
Blundered yet won.

Their weekly thwarting of
Pro-Pottsylvanian
Plots made the Cold War a
Bundle of fun.

Very Tragical Mirth

Avidly-Ovidly,
Thisbe and Pyramus,
Badly confused by a
Leonine brute,

Die at the hands of two
Post-Babylonian
Amateur thespians,
Bottom and Flute.

Filmericks

Rick seems the least moral of men,
But he does noble deeds now and then.
  When another man's wife
  Re-enters his life,
He elects not to play it again.

Says a young lady traveling in Oz,
"The three guys in my life have real floz.
  I've got one who lacks heart,
  One who's not very smart,
One with no balls, which gives a girl poz."

A college grad hears that a plastic
Career would be something fantastic.
  When his girlfriend gets mad
  That he's done like her Dad
With her Mom, his solution is drastic.

Marty's life in the present day sucks
Until Doc Brown's capacitor's flux
  Helps him rewrite the past
  So his father, at last,
Can have confidence, cool, and big bucks.

Locked-up shrink with a keen appetite
Helps the FBI gain fresh insight
  In re odd serial
  Killer material.
But Doc's scheming to bite and take flight.

An IRA fugitive's awed
By a singer's sweet voice and hot bod.
  After she sizes him
  Up, she surprises him.
Turns out she's packing a rod.

You're Yoda's fair-haired Jedi laddie,
While I am the ultimate baddie,
  So this 411
  Will blow your mind, son:
Luke Skywalker, guess who's your Daddy.

Supernatural Sitcoms

The love life of a brave astronaut'll
Be something a blonde babe who's hot'll
  Enhance. She'll entrance
  If she wears harem pants,
Calls him "Master," and lives in a bottle.

Sam sometimes gets into a fix,
Then she fixes things with magic tricks.
  Her husband has no
  Mystic powers, although
He is played by two different Dicks.

Taste and See That the Lord Is Wrathful

"This life loses its salt," declared Lot,
"When the temper of Heaven gets hot.
  Though I played the good host,
  All my neighbors are toast,
And my wife, once so sweet, now is not."

Hairy Sibling Rivalry

One twin, less hirsute than the other,
Is preferred by their crafty old mother,
  Who cons their blind Dad
  Into blessing her lad
Instead of his fuzzier brother.

Zeus on Courtship

I'm a swan, I'm a bull, I'm a shower
Of gold in her lap! Feel the power!
  I woo her, I rape her,
  I even reshape her—
Say, into a cow once I plow her.

Great American Novel Limerick

Huck's a good-hearted boy, but he's white
And has always heard slavery's right,
  Until friendship with Jim
  On a raft causes him
To see things in a whole different light.

Melancholy Danish Limerick

Uncle Claudius got Mom into bed
Via murther, my father's ghost said.
  I'm unsure, but 'tis certain
  That ere Act V's curtain
A whole lot more Danes will be dead.

Anonymous

"If you read it, you'll see that my verse
Is all mediocre or worse,"
  Sighs Edward de Vere.
  "I'm no William Shakespeare,
Notwithstanding the fancies fools nurse."

Balcony Scene

Quoth a lusty young buck from Verona,
"Yon Miss Capulet gives me a bona.
  Since I crashed her Dad's party,
  I've throbbed with a hearty
Desire to be her organ dona."

Muses Juliet, "Untapped and young,
With my hottest love songs yet unsung,
  I thrill to lush words
  About flowers and birds.
Slip me more of sweet Romeo's tongue."

Bard Bio Triptych

The teen son of a Warwickshire glover
Ties the knot with a mid-twenties lover.
  He then drops out of view
  For a few years to do
Stuff that scholars have yet to discover.

Soon, the theatres of London engage
His attention. He writes for the stage.
  There his kings, clowns, and queens,
  His sword fights and love scenes,
Earn him more than an everyday wage.

1613, his playhouse burns down.
He retires to his Avonside town
  To enjoy waning years
  Less unsettled than Lear's,
Then embarks for new realms of renown.

Notes

"Tall Tale": Frank Lloyd Wright's letter to the editor denouncing the Empire State Building appeared in the December 30, 1931, issue of *The Nation*.

"Generations": The author owes an apology to the aunts in his family, who have pointed out that, although they sometimes find him a bit trying, they do not shock easily.

"On a White Conceptual Poet's Performance of Michael Brown's Autopsy Report": Michael Brown is an 18-year old black man who was killed by a white police officer in Ferguson, Missouri, on August 9, 2014. The following year, white poet Kenneth Goldsmith performed "The Body of Michael Brown," a reading consisting of excerpts from the slain man's autopsy report. An account of that event appeared in the October 5, 2015, issue of *The New Yorker*.

"Making Light Among the Tombs": Anthony Hecht was co-editor with John Hollander of the 1967 book *Jiggery-Pokery*, which did so much to popularize the double dactyl. *Flight Among the Tombs* is one collection of Hecht's poems.

"Bedtime Reading": Xaviera Hollander is a Dutch sex worker and author who achieved celebrity with her 1971 memoir *The Happy Hooker*.

"Riyadh Reformer": Mohammed bin Salman, son of King Salman bin Abdulaziz, became Crown Prince of Saudi Arabia in 2017.

"How the West Was Wayne": Marion Morrison is the birth name of the movie star known professionally as John Wayne.

"Good Golly!": Richard Wayne Penniman is the birth name of the musician known professionally as Little Richard.

"Points in Space": The Russian mathematician Nikolai Ivanovich Lobachevsky, in addition to being a character in a Tom Lehrer song, is a major figure in the history of non-Euclidean geometry.

"Moose and Squirrel": Rocket J. ("Rocky") Squirrel and Bullwinkle J. Moose were the animated cartoon stars of the paired television programs *Rocky and His Friends* and *The Bullwinkle Show* (1959-1964). Their antagonists, Boris and Natasha, had Russian names and accents but were presented as spies working for the fictional nation of Pottsylvania.

"Supernatural Sitcoms": Barbara Eden as Jeannie, a sexy genie, and Elizabeth Montgomery as Samantha, a sexy witch, starred in the television programs *I Dream of Jeannie* (1965-1970) and *Bewitched* (1964-1972). Dick York and Dick Sargent both played Samantha's husband in the latter show.

"Filmericks": *Casablanca, The Wizard of Oz, The Graduate, Back to the Future, The Silence of the Lambs, The Crying Game, The Empire Strikes Back.*

About the Author

Chris O'Carroll, author of *The Joke's on Me* (also from White Violet Press), is a *Light* magazine featured poet as well as a contributor to the Potcake Chapbooks series and *The Great American Wise Ass Poetry Anthology*. His poems appear in *An Amaranthine Summer* (published in memory of Kim Bridgford), *Extreme Sonnets*, *Love Affairs at the Villa Nelle,* and *New York City Haiku,* among other collections. Chris is a member of Actors Equity and has performed widely as a stand-up comedian. He lives in Massachusetts with his wife, historian Karen Manners Smith.

www.ingramcontent.com/pod-product-compliance
Lightning Source LLC
Chambersburg PA
CBHW032009080426
42735CB00007B/550